Troubleshooting AWS Glue Job Failures

Table of Contents

Chapter 1. Introduction

Navigating through a digital forest may often lead to unforeseen complications, even for the most experienced adventurers. Technical yet demystifying, this Special Report focuses on the process of troubleshooting AWS Glue Job Failures, a task that has befuddled many professionals over time. With the aims and objectives crystal clear, this report sheds light on the nuances of AWS Glue, intersects with job failure scenarios, and finally lands on resolutions, ensuring a smooth journey. So, tighten your seatbelts as we traverse through the land of AWS Glue job failures, promising to transform your confusion into comprehension, and your troubleshooting worries into robust solutions.

Chapter 2. Understanding AWS Glue Fundamentals

Amazon Web Services (AWS) Glue has become a catchphrase within the realm of cloud-based data processing services for several reasons. Created to facilitate the seamless extraction, transformation, and loading (ETL) of data, AWS Glue uses Apache Spark and Python to accomplish this task. In AWS Glue, jobs comprise the core business logic, making them the central part of the service.

Let's begin by understanding AWS Glue's primary components and how they intertwine to streamline the task of ETL.

2.1. AWS Glue Components

AWS Glue consists of three primary components:

1. AWS Glue Data Catalog

2. AWS Glue ETL Engine

3. Flexible Job Scheduler

AWS Glue Data Catalog is a persistent metadata repository store that is compatible with Apache Hive Metastore. AWS Glue Data Catalog provides a unified view of your data spread across different AWS services. It is inbuilt, eliminating the need for an external metadata repository, which can be expensive and complicated to set up and maintain.

AWS Glue ETL Engine is powered by Apache Spark, a fast, in-memory data processing engine with elegant and expressive development APIs to enable data workers to efficiently execute streaming, machine learning, or SQL workloads that require fast iterative access to their datasets.

Flexible Job Scheduler allows scheduling of jobs on demand, job chaining, and job bookmarking. On-demand scheduling allows jobs to be started without explicitly defining when the job should run. Job chaining involves setting up a series of jobs where each job completes and triggers the next. Job bookmarking enables AWS Glue to keep track of data that has already been processed during a previous run of an ETL job. This allows Glue jobs to process incremental data on subsequent runs.

2.2. AWS Glue Jobs

In the context of AWS Glue, a job is a business logic unit that performs the ETL task. You create a job in your AWS Glue console, choosing the necessary script or writing one in Python. AWS Glue uses this script to move data between your source and target data stores.

2.3. Understanding Crawlers

Crawlers are another critical component of AWS Glue. AWS Glue uses crawlers to connect to your source or target data store, extract metadata, and create table definitions in the AWS Glue Data Catalog. A crawler connects to a data store, progresses through a prioritized list of classifiers to determine the schema for your data, and then creates metadata tables in the AWS Glue Data Catalog.

2.4. Python Shell Jobs and Python Library

Python shell jobs in AWS Glue are for scenarios where your ETL job is resource-intensive and doesn't need Spark, or involves procedural Python ETL jobs like zipping and unzipping files, downloading data from the web, and transforming data into a form compatible with relational databases.

AWS Glue also provides a library containing classes to create dynamic frames, sources, sinks, and transformations. The `GlueContext` class is your entry point and connects your job to your data sources, data targets, and transformations.

2.5. Security and Access Control

Equally vital is the way AWS Glue treats security—by managing it through AWS Identity and Access Management (IAM) roles. Once you create a role for AWS Glue, it defines the AWS resources that your job can access during execution. IAM policies govern the operations that can be performed on the AWS resources.

Mastering of these fundamentals intricately ties to understanding AWS Glue Job Failures, their genesis, and resolution. A careful consideration of every aspect from creating a dataset, mobilizing a crawler, structuring a job, or determining the security constraints will breed an impeccable grasp over handling AWS Glue and the unpredictable occurrences of job failures.

Navigating the forest of AWS Glue may seem like a complex task. But by taking a broad view and understanding these underlying components, you can begin to see the lay of the land. Each element plays a role in how AWS Glue functions, and together, they form a cohesive mechanism to manage your data seamlessly. Understanding these fundamentals creates the foundation for identifying and resolving issues when a job failure scenario arises.

Chapter 3. Exploring AWS Glue Job Failures

AWS Glue, an end-to-end data integration service, helps extract, transform, and load (ETL) vast amounts of data from multiple sources for analytics. While its serverless, pay-as-you-go nature is appealing, one must navigate its complexities to avoid job failures effectively.

3.1. Understanding AWS Glue

The first rung on our ladder to mastery involves understanding AWS Glue in a closer, more detailed manner. AWS Glue is part of the larger AWS ecosystem and seamlessly integrates with other services, making life easier for data scientists and engineers. But, like anything else, it throws occasional curveballs, such as Glue job failures.

AWS Glue's magic lies in its ETL capabilities, which allow it to populate data lakes, data warehouses, and other repositories. It discovers and catalogs metadata, generates Python or Scala code automatically to translate different data formats, and handles resources during runtime.

3.2. AWS Glue Components

Before exploring failures, it's essential we familiarize ourselves with AWS Glue's components.

- Glue Catalog: The centralized metadata repository termed as the 'Persistent Metadata Store'.

- Glue Crawlers: These work with the Catalog and are responsible for database and table creation.

- Glue Jobs and Glue ETL: The core components that handle the extraction, transformation, and loading of data.

- Glue Data Catalog: The go-to querying point with Glue creating and inferring schemas, storing and retrieving table metadata.

3.3. AWS Glue Job Failures: An Overview

Even with knowledge of Glue's components, professionals might come across job failure. Job failure can occur due to many reasons, such as insufficient memory, script errors, timeout, misconfiguration, and more. In the subsequent section, we will understand these failures in detail.

3.4. Understanding AWS Glue Job Failure Reasons

Let's dive deeper into the various reasons AWS Glue jobs can fail:

- Time Out: AWS Glue jobs have a default timeout limit of 2880 minutes (48 hours). If a job runs for a longer duration, it times out, and hence, it fails.

- Memory: Insufficient memory can cause job failures. When a job exceeds its allocated memory, it is terminated.

- Incorrect ETL Scripts: Scripts with incorrect syntax, missing libraries, or inaccurate data definitions can lead to failure.

- Configuration Issues: Misconfiguration in the AWS Glue job parameters, Security Groups, Virtual Private Cloud (VPC) can lead to job failure.

- Dependency-Related Issues: AWS Glue heavily relies on underlying AWS Services. Any problem in these services can impact Glue jobs.

- Data-Related Issues: Issues like inconsistent or incorrect data types in the source and the target, data skewness can cause Glue Job failures.

3.5. Key Steps for AWS Glue Job Failure Troubleshooting

To effectively troubleshoot AWS Glue Job failures, one must follow structured steps. Let's delve into each:

1. Identify the Job Failure Error: Start by identifying the failure error by logging into the AWS Glue Console, clicking on Jobs, and choosing the failing job's name. Under the History tab, select the Job Run ID of the failed job. Here, you'll find the Error message which gives you a clue about the cause of failure.

2. Investigate the Error: Once you have the error message, it's time to investigate. The AWS Glue Developer Guide and AWS Discussion Forums can be helpful resources to understand the meaning of specific error messages.

3. Check Glue Job Logs: Glue Job logs provide detailed insight into the job execution, making them a critical resource for troubleshooting. Logs are maintained in AWS CloudWatch.

4. Adjust the Configuration Parameters: Post the error identification and understanding, you may need to adjust job configurations such as allocated memory and timeout duration.

5. Debug and Modify the ETL Script: Use careful debugging and consequent modifications to correct script-related errors. AWS Glue's interface allows you to test and rectify your scripts.

3.6. Best Practices for Avoiding AWS Glue Job Failures

Prevention is certainly a better strategy than rectification. Following are some best practices to avoid job failures:

1. Monitor Job Executions: Regularly monitoring job execution lets you identify and rectify potential issues earlier.

2. Right-Sizing Resources: Allocating appropriate resources (CPU, memory) can help prevent timeout and out of memory errors.

3. Periodically Validate Your ETL Scripts: Regularly checking your ETL Scripts for errors can help avert failures.

4. Optimally Configure Job Parameters: It is essential to accurately define the timeout limits, maximum capacity parameters, and worker types.

3.7. conclusion

While AWS Glue automates the resource administration and code creation, its use does come with breakdowns, primarily job failures. However, having a deep understanding of Glue's architecture and the causes of these failures - along with a structured troubleshooting approach - you equip yourself to combat these mishaps effectively. Keep in mind; it's a continuous learning process. As you get more familiar with AWS Glue, troubleshoot errors, and apply preventive measures, your journey through the digital forest becomes more comfortable.

In this context, understand that failures are not setbacks but steppingstones to learning and sharpening your AWS Glue skills. Therefore, on the road to mastering AWS Glue Job Failures, always remember the adage, 'What Doesn't Kill You, Makes You Stronger.'

Chapter 4. Data Preparation: An Essential Step

Data preparation is fundamental to the successful execution of an AWS Glue job. This phase involves gathering, cleaning, and organizing data for analysis or use by the Glue job. Failure in this stage can impede either the creation or the execution of an AWS Glue job. A well-prepared dataset aids in extracting meaningful insights and ensures that Glue scripts run smoothly.

4.1. Understanding Data Sources

The first step to successful data preparation involves identifying and understanding the nature of your data sources. AWS Glue can ingest data from a variety of sources such as Amazon S3, Amazon RDS, and Amazon Redshift. Each of these sources may use different data formats like CSV, JSON, or Parquet, affecting how you prepare and process the data.

Reviewing the data source and understanding its format is crucial. While AWS Glue has a built-in feature known as "Crawlers" for schema detection, it is not infallible. It is critical abidingly to review and correct the schema if necessary.

4.2. Data Cleaning

Data in its raw form may contain outlying data points, errors, duplicate entries, and missing values, causing a phenomenon known as "dirty data". Dirty data can lead to incorrect analysis results and AWS Glue Job failures. Therefore, it is critical to clean your dataset thoroughly before running AWS Glue jobs. Cleaning includes processes such as de-duplicating data, rectifying incorrect entries, handling missing data, and removing irrelevant data points.

For example, when dealing with missing values, consider whether to fill in the gaps using interpolation or imputation methods, or to omit these records entirely. The choice depends on the nature of your dataset and the context in which the data missing.

4.3. Feature Selection and Engineering

One of the biggest challenges in data preparation pertains to determining which attributes or features of the data should be included in the final dataset for analysis. Inappropriate feature selection can lead to models that do not accurately represent the data's underlying structure, resulting in faulty insights.

Feature engineering, on the other hand, allows creation of new features based on existing ones which can be invaluable in machine learning scenarios. AWS Glue can help you with transformation and generation of such features using various AWS Glue transformations available in Glue ETL jobs.

4.4. Schema Evolution

One important aspect to keep in mind while preparing your data is schema evolution — changes that occur to a dataset's schema over time. AWS Glue has a schema evolution feature that can help handle this challenge, but it's critical to monitor and manage this effectively to avoid job failures. This is especially relevant in scenarios where your AWS Glue ETL jobs become dependent on specific schema arrangements that evolve over time.

4.5. Data Partitioning

Data partitioning is a vital strategy when dealing with large datasets. It optimizes job performance by dividing a large dataset into smaller, more manageable components based on certain criteria such as date or range of values. AWS Glue supports partitioning while reading data, which can drastically reduce the amount of data read during an ETL job, improving efficiency and speed of the job.

If partitioning is not addressed adequately during the data preparation phase, it can lead to less than ideal job performance or even job failures. Therefore, a comprehensive understanding of your data size and structure is necessary to identify the most suitable partitioning strategy.

4.6. Conclusion

Data preparation is an essential yet often overlooked phase in the AWS Glue job process. Thorough preparation not only helps prevent job failures, but also improves overall job efficiency and delivers more accurate insights. By acknowledging and embracing the complexities of the data preparation process, you can turn potential pitfalls into opportunities for robust data analysis.

Chapter 5. Debugging AWS Glue: An Intuitive Approach

Let's begin with an overview: AWS Glue is an extensively used managed extract, transform, and load (ETL) service that makes it easy for users to prepare and load their data for analytics. However, AWS Glue users might encounter job failures, leading to a disruption in workflow and data flow. The key to overcoming these challenges lies in accurate and efficient debugging. Thus, we present an intuitive approach to debugging AWS Glue job failures.

5.1. Understanding AWS Glue Job Failures

Before delving into how to resolve AWS Glue job failures, understanding the possible reasons behind these issues is of equal importance. AWS Glue job failures can be broadly categorized into: failures due to design issues, execution issues, and resource-related issues.

Design issues revolve around problems in the job's design, mainly in its scripts or the workflow structure. Meanwhile, execution problems arise due to the issues in runtime environment like missing or inaccessible data sources, incorrect output directory, or unsuccessful executions of certain operations of the script.

Resource-related issues involve failure due to inadequate resources provided for the AWS Glue job. As the data size and complexity of operations increase, a job may need more resources than it has, leading to failure.

5.2. Troubleshooting Design and Execution Issues

The error messages that AWS Glue returns may help in diagnosing the issues. For instance, you can retrieve error logs from Amazon CloudWatch Logs for a failed job run and examine the stack trace for the job to determine the cause of the failure.

If the error is in the script, Glue's script editor can be used to correct the issue. Make sure to validate the script after making changes.

In case of execution issues, check if the source or target is available and correctly defined. Incorrect input or output paths can be a common cause of execution errors. Be sure to verify the connection and access to these data sources to prevent such errors.

5.3. Tackling Resource-Related Issues

Resource-related issues commonly arise due to inadequate provisioning of job resources. To debug this, you need to determine if your job has enough memory and CPU resources to process data.

One way around this issue is to increase the maximum capacity or job concurrency. Adjust these values according to the data size and the complexity of the operations involved.

You can use the AWS Glue job metrics available in CloudWatch to monitor your job's resource utilization. AWS CloudWatch provides important metrics such as 'Memory', 'CPU Utilization', and 'Job Capacity' that allow you to understand resource usage and diagnose resource-related issues.

5.4. Delving Into Common Errors and Resolutions

Certain failure cases have common causes and therefore solutions. A detailed understanding of such commonly occurring errors will sharpen your debugging skills.

One such example is Timeout errors. Timeout occurs when a job run exceeds the maximum execution time. An efficient solution to this problem is increasing the job 'Timeout property' to ensure that your job has ample running time to execute.

Misconfigured source or target paths, invalid script references, and resource capacity errors are other examples of common errors. The solutions typically involve correcting the configuration, valid referencing, and adjusting the capacity, respectively.

5.5. Enhancing Proficiency with Best Practices

Preventing job failures by following a series of best practices can enhance your debugging proficiency. These include proper planning and preparation, regular monitoring of jobs, and thorough testing during development. Further, keeping track of the AWS Glue job runtime logs and metrics, and understanding the nuances of capacity management, can keep job failures at bay.

In conclusion, understanding the reasons for job failures, coupled with proficient use of best practices and utilization of the right AWS tools, can significantly minimize AWS Glue job failures. At the same time, it equips one with the skill to quickly resolve any unforeseen issues that may arise, thus paving the way for efficient data processing and analytics.

Chapter 6. Walkthrough of Common AWS Glue Job Errors

AWS Glue is an intuitive and robust tool that can occasionally throw a curveball in the form of job failures. However, these peculiar complications or errors aren't indecipherable, as they might initially seem. They simply require a deeper understanding and systematic approach to unravel their mysteries.

6.1. Error: Glue Job Timeout

Arguably the most common AWS Glue job failure is a job timeout. This occurs when your job runs for a longer time than the maximum job timeout limit, which is set to 2880 minutes (48 hours) by default.

It's crucial to first identify the reasons behind your abnormal job run time. Here are a few potential causes:

- Large dataset: If your job is processing a massive dataset, it might naturally take more time than expected.

- Inefficient scripts: An inefficient or poorly optimized ETL script could also lead to extended run times.

- Inadequate resources: If the compute resources allocated to perform the job are inadequate, the job might run longer than expected. For instance, fewer DPUs than needed could be a possible cause.

To address this issue:

1. Increase your job timeout: If your job naturally requires more time due to its complexity or the size of the data it's processing,

consider increasing the maximum job timeout.

2. Optimize your script: In many cases, optimizing your ETL script can drastically reduce the job's running time.

3. Increase resources: Depending on the nature of your job, you might need to allocate more DPUs to it.

6.2. Error: Glue Job Out of Memory

Another common error in Glue jobs is the 'Out of Memory' error. This error arises when your job attempts to use more memory than is available. An excessively large dataset, complex or memory-intensive operations, and inadequate resources could be the possible causes of this error.

Here are some tips to resolve this issue:

1. Increase resources: This is the most straightforward solution – increase the memory available for your Glue job by increasing the number of DPUs or choosing a worker type with more memory.

2. Optimize your script: More complex operations and inefficient code could be consuming excess memory. Try optimizing your ETL script to reduce memory usage.

3. Distribute data processing: If you're processing a large dataset, consider splitting your job to process the data in smaller chunks.

6.3. Error: Access Denied

Access denied messages occur when your Glue job tries to access a resource for which it has inadequate permissions. This is typically related to IAM roles and access policies.

To debug this error, consider the following possibilities:

1. Insufficient IAM permissions: Check the IAM role associated with your Glue job. Does it have the necessary permissions to perform the task?

2. Incorrect resource URI: Check the URI of the resource that your job is trying to access. Is it correct and up-to-date?

3. Encryption issues: If the resource is encrypted, does the Glue job have the necessary keys and permissions to decrypt it?

4. Resource modifications: Has there been any recent modifications in the resource's access permissions?

These errors can be fixed by updating IAM roles and policies, correcting resource URIs, dealing with encryption issues, and tracking resource modifications.

6.4. Error: Connection Timeouts

Connection timeouts happen when your job fails to establish a connection with a resource in a specified time period.

Here's how you can fix this:

1. Security group settings: Check the inbound and outbound rules of the security group attached to the resource.

2. Network issues: General network problems could be a cause of connection issues. Check your network configuration and connectivity.

3. Resource errors: If the resource is not available or is under heavy load, it could lead to timeouts.

To resolve these, modify security group settings, rectify network issues, or address the problematic resource.

In conclusion, AWS Glue job errors often emerge due to a myriad of reasons - ranging from resource inadequacy to scripting inefficiencies or even simply, time lapses. Understanding these complexities is key to deciphering these errors. With a keen eye and penchant for diagnosis, one can sail smoothly through these errors, fixing them as they come, and ensuring a seamless ETL process.

Chapter 7. Directory of AWS Glue Error Codes

AWS Glue, a fully-managed extract, transform, and load (ETL) service, is ideally designed to categorize your data, clean it, enrich it, and move it reliably between various data stores. However, its comprehensive nature may sometimes lead to a wide array of error messages, each signifying a unique problem. In this chapter, we aim to provide a detailed directory of AWS Glue Error Codes, along with potential reasons and optimal solutions.

7.1. ERROR 001: Unable to Access Data Store

This error is encountered when AWS Glue fails to access the data store defined in your job. It can be due to many reasons, such as incorrect connection properties, inaccessible data locations, data store downtime, or insufficient permissions.

To troubleshoot, first, verify that your input and output connections are correct. If accessing a database, ensure it is up and available. If it's a file-based data store, check the path for any typos. Make sure the AWS Glue service role has the necessary permissions to access the data store.

7.2. ERROR 002: Unable to Write to Target

This error can occur if AWS Glue could not write to the output target specified in your job. The common causes include write permissions issues, insufficient disk space, incompatible data schema, or transient network issues.

Double-check the AWS IAM permissions for the AWS Glue service role to ensure it has the necessary write permissions. If writing to a disk-based service like S3, ensure there is sufficient disk space. Check for schema incompatibilities between your source and target. Finally, if it's a transient network issue, retry the job.

7.3. ERROR 003: OutOfMemory Error

This error occurs if the ETL job exceeds the maximum allocated Java heap size. It can be due to processing large datasets or issues in your script leading to inefficient memory usage.

Try to optimize your script for efficient memory usage. If your job is processing large datasets, consider increasing the Glue job's compute resources. For complex ETL tasks, consider enabling job bookmarking to keep track of data that the job has already processed.

7.4. ERROR 004: Timeout Error

This error is encountered when a job runs longer than the specified timeout period. It could be due to inefficient script execution, large data set processing, or external system latencies.

First, optimize your ETL script for efficiency. If your job works on large datasets or depends on external systems, try to increase the timeout limit. For jobs dependent on other systems, look for possible latencies and work on resolving them.

7.5. ERROR 005: Job Bookmark Error

This error often occurs when the job bookmarking feature is misconfigured. AWS Glue uses job bookmarks to track data that it has already processed in previous runs of an ETL job.

Verify the configuration settings of job bookmarking. Ensure that

AWS Glue has the necessary permissions to write job bookmarks.

These are just a few examples of common AWS Glue job failure error codes. Each code corresponds to a specific issue, and understanding them can greatly ease the process of failure diagnosis and repair. Having this directory at hand will not only cut short your troubleshooting time but also empower you to make the most of AWS Glue.

Chapter 8. Practical Solutions to Common AWS Glue Job Failures

Let's dive right into the mix by identifying the most common AWS Glue Job Failures and exploring practical solutions to these conundrums.

8.1. Understanding AWS Glue Jobs

AWS Glue is a fully managed ETL service that prepares and loads your data for analysis. However, even with its considerable capabilities, AWS Glue jobs can fail due to various reasons - memory issues, timeouts, data mismatches, and so forth. Understanding AWS Glue job types and their intricacies can set the stage for us to delve into their troubleshooting.

There are two types of AWS Glue jobs - the Python shell jobs and the Spark job. Python shell jobs are meant for small-scale ETL tasks with a runtime limitation of 48 hours. On the other hand, Glue Spark jobs are designed for large datasets and can run indefinitely.

8.2. Common AWS Glue Job Failures and Solutions

In this section, we will shed light on some of the most common AWS Glue Job failures and provide you with detailed solutions to help you successfully run your ETL jobs.

8.2.1. Job Run Timeouts

One of the most common reasons for job failure is job run timeouts. A Glue ETL job times out when the execution of the job exceeds the specified timeout value.

Solution: It's quite simple to address this. You can increase the timeout value within the job parameters to surpass the current job runtime. If further timeouts occur, consider revising job resource allocations or optimizing the scripts for better performance.

8.2.2. Out of Memory Issues

Memory issues are another source of Glue job failures. When the ETL script consumes more memory than allocated, the job breaks down, yielding the 'Out of Memory' error.

Solution: There are two approaches to address this issue. One, you can optimize your ETL scripts, carefully evaluating memory utilization. The second solution would be to increase the maximum capacity of the job, to fit the job's memory needs.

8.2.3. Insufficient Concurrent DPUs

DPUs (Data Processing Units) essentially determine the resources allocated to an AWS Glue job. If your Glue job demands more DPUs than assigned, it would inevitably lead to a failure.

Solution: AWS allows you to increase the number of DPUs allotted to your job. However, the primary action point would be understanding the resource needs of your job and allocating DPUs accordingly.

8.2.4. Data Mismatch Errors

Data Mismatch Errors occur when there are inconsistencies or issues with the source data, schema mismatches, or incorrect input formats.

Solution: Rectify the mismatch by checking the schema and ensuring that it matches the source data structure. Besides, verify the input format - incorrect or unsupported formats can disrupt Glue job executions.

8.2.5. Job Bookmarking Issues

Job bookmarking issues generally occur if the source dataset is considerably large, leading to performance and job failure issues.

Solution: If you observe slower run times with large datasets, consider disabling the job bookmarks. With the job bookmarking feature disabled, AWS Glue processes the entire dataset whenever the job runs.

8.3. AWS Glue Error Handling

Alongside the common failure scenarios and their solutions, it's also crucial to understand how AWS Glue manages error handling. AWS Glue is designed to transit into failure state if the script throws a non-retryable exception or exhausts the number of retries. It is advisable to incorporate error handling within your scripts to minimize the risk of job failure.

Remember, proper utilization of logs, script reviews, job bookmark configurations, and memory management are just as significant as understanding AWS Glue job failure issues.

8.4. Conclusion

While it can be challenging to troubleshoot AWS Glue Job failures, a systematic approach, coupled with a detailed understanding of the AWS landscape, the Glue ETL service, and its common issues, can help resolve these obstacles. Keep this guide in your toolkit as you navigate through your AWS Glue journey, as it can well be an aid in debugging and optimizing your Glue jobs.

In the end, troubleshooting is not about finding quick fixes; instead, it's about understanding the problem at hand more intimately, learning from it, and developing robust preemptive measures for future encounters. So, venture forth with this newfound knowledge and tackle those AWS Glue Job failures head on!

Chapter 9. Performance Optimization: Best Practices in AWS Glue

AWS Glue is indeed a powerful serverless ETL service that makes it easy to move data between your data stores. However, performance optimization is crucial to ensure your AWS Glue jobs run smoothly and without needless cost. Thorough understanding of the best practices is indispensable for anyone seeking to efficiently navigate this digital landscape.

9.1. Understanding AWS Glue

Before digging into performance enhancement techniques, let's get a grasp on some AWS Glue basics. AWS Glue is a fully managed extract, transform, and load (ETL) service that makes it easy for users to prepare and load their data for analytics. AWS Glue discovers your data and stores the associated metadata (like table definition and schema) in the AWS Glue Data Catalog. Once cataloged, your data is immediately searchable, queryable, and available for ETL.

9.2. Data Partitioning

Data partitioning is one of the fundamental ways to optimize your AWS Glue jobs. In AWS Glue, data partitioning works by dividing your data into smaller, more manageable parts called partitions. AWS Glue is designed to work with data stored in Amazon S3 buckets, where it makes the most of Amazon S3's partitioning features to read and write data faster.

To take full advantage of partitioning, make sure your data is partitioned before creating your Glue ETL jobs. This helps AWS Glue access only the relevant parts of your data, reducing the amount of data read, and hence, improving the performance and efficiency of your jobs. Remember, partitioning columns with high cardinality, such as timestamps, can ingest your data faster into the AWS Glue Data Catalog.

9.3. Job Script Optimization

Job script optimization involves tweaking your scripts to speed up job performance. Consider using Python or Scala shell jobs which do not involve Apache Spark, for light transformations, as they tend to be quicker than Spark ETL jobs (which are better fit for heavy transformations).

Also, AWS Glue uses lazy evaluation, where transformations are not immediately performed as they're read from left to right in your script. Instead, they're stacked until an action is required, leading to delays. You can bypass this by forcing transformations to be executed immediately using methods like `repartition` or `checkpoint`, each with its own use cases and performance impact.

9.4. Reducing Query Runtime

Profiling your SQL queries is a good way of identifying potential performance issues that can be optimized. It's advisable to reduce query runtime by filtering, aggregating, or reducing your data before a join, rather than after. AWS Glue also supports predicate pushdown, where it filters the data on read tasks, reducing the volume of data shuffled or spilled to disk.

Consider using hash joins instead of sort merge joins. While sort merge joins process larger datasets, they need more memory and are slower due to the needed sorting. Hash joins, although requiring all the records of a smaller dataset to be in memory, tend to be faster.

9.5. Fine-tuning Data Formats

Different data formats have unique performance characteristics. The best format for your AWS Glue jobs largely depends on the nature and volume of your data. Parquet and ORC are columnar formats that significantly speed up column-based queries and save costs. They're preferable when working with big data, as they support advanced features like compression and schema evolution.

CSV, JSON and Avro, on the other hand, are row-based formats suitable for data that doesn't require many computations or aggregations.

9.6. Maximizing Resource Utilization

You can adjust the resources allocated to your AWS Glue jobs to get the best performance. The `Max Capacity` parameter sets the maximum number of data processing units (DPUs) that can be consumed by a job run. The more DPUs you allocate, the more parallel tasks your Spark environment will be able to handle.

However, use caution while increasing DPUs as allocating too many can result in additional charges. To manage this, AWS Glue offers a `job timeout property`, which terminates a job if it runs longer than the specified time frame, saving you from unexpected costs.

9.7. Job Bookmarking and Concurrency

Job bookmarking helps to ensure Glue jobs process each data set only once. It keeps track of the data that has been processed during previous job runs by storing state information. If a job fails, this state information helps Glue resume from the point of failure. This prevents re-processing of old data and saves compute resources.

AWS Glue supports concurrent ETL job execution, which can significantly reduce job runtime. If there are tasks that do not depend on other tasks, it's beneficial to run them concurrently. You can use the 'Max concurrent runs' option to specify the maximum number of concurrent runs allowed for a job.

9.8. Monitoring with AWS CloudWatch

Monitoring your AWS Glue jobs provides vital insights into job performance and its impact on your data processing pipeline. AWS CloudWatch offers robust metrics and logs that help monitor job performance and diagnose issues. From tracking DPU utilization, job run times to data bytes read or written, CloudWatch keeps you informed about the health of your jobs.

In conclusion, achieving performance optimization in AWS Glue involves understanding the service, partitioning data appropriately, optimizing scripts and queries, choosing the right data formats, maximizing resource utilization, leveraging job bookmarking/concurrency, and finally, instituting a monitoring system. By implementing these best practices, you'll be ready to tackle AWS Glue job troubleshooting with confidence and precision.

Chapter 10. Advanced Troubleshooting Techniques for AWS Glue Jobs

As you venture further into the prosaic wilderness of AWS Glue job failures, it's imperative to understand and master advanced troubleshooting techniques. A proficient adventurer knows that building an arsenal of sophisticated problem-solving tools is instrumental in surviving the thickets of technological challenges.

10.1. Understanding AWS Glue Job Failures

AWS Glue, an essential tool in the AWS suite, is a fully managed extract, transform, and load (ETL) service that simplifies the process of moving data between diverse data stores. However, with great capabilities come complex challenges, one of which is AWS Glue job failures. These failures can arise from various aspects; sometimes, they are as straightforward as rejecting a misconfigured parameter, while on other occasions, they veil themselves in cryptic error messages.

AWS Glue logs all its activities on CloudWatch, a monitoring service provided by AWS. This log is your guide, the compass that steers you through these hazy terrains. All errors, warnings, and informational statements during the job execution are captured and logged here. Therefore, it's the primary source of information for troubleshooting.

10.2. Addressing Common Error Types

To chart a clear path through the maelstrom of potential AWS Glue job failures, let's start by addressing some common error types and their solutions.

1. `Out of Memory Errors`: This is one of the most frequent errors encountered. It denotes that your job has hit a snag because it's attempting to process a chunk of data larger than the available memory. Adjusting the 'maxCapacity' parameter or increasing the Data Processing Units (DPUs) can serve as a quick fix.

2. `Timeout Errors`: If a job runs for an excessively long time and exceeds the 'timeout' value, it yields a timeout error. The default timeout value is 2880 minutes (48 hours), but it's adjustable per job demand.

3. `Mismatched data schema errors`: If your source and target schemas do not align, AWS Glue jobs can fail. It is thereby vital to ensure that the provided schema is accurate and corresponds with the data. Python Shell Jobs provide a Schema Discovery feature to avoid such issues.

4. `Concurrency Errors`: This signifies you have hit the concurrency limit for the type of operation attempted. To mitigate such errors, you can adjust the number of parallel jobs running – consider using Job bookmarks for managing jobs efficiently.

10.3. Deep Dive into Log Analysis

Let's understand how to dissect the logs from CloudWatch to identify the root cause of failures. These logs are categorized into system logs and job-run logs.

1. System logs primarily contain information regarding life-cycle

events of specific Glue Job components, like Spark driver, Spark Executor, etc.

2. Job run logs contain more detailed execution traces and exception back traces.

However, to navigate this mass of logs efficiently, the right technique involves searching for the terms 'ERROR' or 'Exception'. Python Shell Jobs logs also do support 'log4j' log levels, thereby facilitating fine control over logging verbosity.

10.4. Implementing Retry Logic

If bad rows or connectivity issues cause the job failure, implementing retry logic can be a robust solution. Based on the failover needs, jobs can be set to automatically restart a certain number of times.

Furthermore, robust error handling and management are integral to avoid the cascade of halts from interfering with the entire AWS Glue ETL flow.

10.5. Profiling and Debugging

Profiling and debugging play enormous roles in tackling job failures. AWS Glue Studio Debugging Panel provides an intuitive interface that presents key job metrics meticulously. Job profiles can identify resource usage, which can, in turn, provide insights into optimization.

In conclusion, traversing the digital labyrinth of AWS Glue jobs requires a holistic understanding of the common error types, diving deep into the log analysis, implementing retry logic, and utilizing debugging tools. Troubleshooting AWS Glue jobs is a daunting task, but with the right tools and understanding, you can transform this bewildering maze into a walk in the park. Remember, every journey begins with a single step. You've embarked on an incredibly exciting journey that will undoubtedly enrich your debugging skills and transform the way you view AWS Glue. Happy troubleshooting!

Chapter 11. Future Insights: Preventing AWS Glue Job Failures

In an increasingly digital landscape, proactive strategies often triumph over reactive approaches. The ability to anticipate problems and implement timely precautions can invariably improve productivity and agility. This chapter focuses on this aspect, with a special emphasis on preventing AWS Glue Job Failures before they occur.

11.1. Understanding the Roots of Common Failures

In order to mitigate potential job failures, it helps first to comprehend common problems and their root causes. A majority of AWS Glue Job Failures can be attributed to three typical trouble spots:

1. Configuration Errors: These occur when the configuration settings for AWS Glue jobs are incorrect or incompatible. They can stem from incorrect input or output data sources, faulty job parameters, or incompatible job scripts.

2. Resource Constraints: Over-utilized system resources like memory, CPU, and network can lead to job failures. This could arise from insufficiently provisioned resources for the volume of data being processed.

3. Data-related Issues: Discrepancies, inconsistencies, or bad quality in source data often result in AWS Glue job failures. For instance, dealing with data that fails data-type validation or surpasses data volume expectations may contribute to job failures.

Taking these factors into account, let's delve into preventative strategies that foresee these problems.

11.2. Preventing Configuration Errors

Taking the time to verify the settings during configuration can be a game-changer. Some preventative measures in this category are:

1. Confirm Source and Target Paths: Ensure that the input and output data sources specified during configuration are valid and accessible by your AWS Glue job. Wrong or inaccessible paths can lead to job failure. Also, ensure that your input data is compatible with the chosen classifier for the job.

2. Validate Script and Job Parameters: Before running a job, always validate the job parameters and scripts for any syntactical or logical errors. Ensure that the job scripts are compatible with the version of AWS Glue you're using. Check the data source types are also compatible.

3. Set Accurate Memory and Timeouts: Allocate appropriate amounts of memory, and set feasible timeout periods for your jobs to prevent them from stalling or failing. Configuring these parameters based on historical data, such as previous job runs, can provide a ballpark figure to start.

11.3. Managing Resource Constraints

Resource-related failures are often a consequence of inappropriate resource allocation or overburdening the system. Here are some preventive strategies:

1. Right-Size Your Resource Allocation: Evaluate the resources your

job requires based on factors like data volume, complexity of the operations, and concurrency needs. Ensure you're not underestimating these factors to prevent your resources from getting overutilized.

2. Enable Job Monitoring: Enabling CloudWatch monitoring for your AWS Glue jobs can give you visibility into the resource parameters like CPU usage, Memory usage, and network throughput. This can help identify constraints before they lead to job failures.

3. Appropriately Partition Your Data: Data partitioning can influence the effective use of resources during job execution. Partitioning your data optimally allows parallel processing and therefore the efficient use of resources.

11.4. Addressing Data-related Issues

Healthy, consistent, and valid data contributes significantly to the successful execution of AWS Glue jobs. Some measures that could be undertaken are:

1. Validate Data Consistency: Regularly validate the consistency, structure, and quality of your source data. Implement data validation measures at each stage of your data pipeline, from ingestion to processing.

2. Normalize Data Types: Ensure all source data adheres to a standard datatype policy. Incorporate datatype conversion provisions in your job scripts where necessary.

3. Strategize Error Handling: Account for potential data errors at the designing stage by developing a robust error handling strategy. This could include actions like skipping or reporting bad data rows and retry strategies in case of failures.

11.5. Incorporating Autoregressive Predictive Maintenance

Aside from these specific strategies, the application of predictive analytics can also further preventative endeavors. Autoregressive predictive maintenance is one such approach. Leveraging machine learning, it forecasts job failures based on historical patterns and indicators. Autoscaling reactively increases or decreases resource allocation based on real-time demand. While it doesn't prevent a failure, it does hasten recovery, minimizing downtime.

Preventing AWS Glue job failures isn't just about a one-off setup but a continuous improvement process that involves monitoring, performance tuning, and optimization. By bringing foresight into your AWS Glue job preparations, you can not only pre-empt failures but also vastly improve the reliability and performance of your tasks. Failure may not be entirely avoidable but being prepared can make a significant difference in minimizing their occurrence or mitigating their impact.